DADDY'S MINI-ME

By Arnold Henry
Illustrated by Ted M. Sandiford

Piton Books

D1164921

CALGARY PUBLIC LIBRARY

FEB   2019

The Inspiration

After the birth of my son, I decided to take a year off work so that I could capture every moment of his life. Daddy's Mini-Me was created based on these proud and special moments that I was able to witness during his early developmental stages.

Daddy's Mini-Me by Arnold Henry
Illustrated by Ted M. Sandiford
Edited by Tracy Blaine & Melinda R. Cordell

Text copyright © 2018 by Arnold Henry

Printed in China

Published 2018 by Piton Books, Chestermere, Alberta, Canada. All rights reserved. No part of this publication may be reproduced, stored in a retrieval system, or transmitted in any form or by any means, electronic, mechanical, recording or otherwise, without the prior written permission of Piton Books.

The Cataloguing-in-Publication Data is on file at Library and Archives Canada

ISBN: 978-0-9940272-6-9

Learn more about us and our story at
www.daddysminime.com

For all the proud fathers who continue
to be present in their children's lives.

Hello fathers,
by signing this agreement below, you have made a
promise to always be a role model for your child or children.

I, _____,
promise to be the best father in the world to my
beautiful and amazing child/children,

_____.

Print Name: _____

Signature: _____

Daddy and Baby meet
for the first time.
"Wow," says Daddy.
"My Baby looks like a mini-me."

As time goes by,
Baby does what Baby sees.
Daddy is looking
as proud as can be.
My Baby acts just like me.

Daddy, Daddy, look at me!
I can smile when you smile at me.

I am looking.

I can see.

You can smile just like me.

Go...Go...Go my mini-me.

Daddy, Daddy, look at me!
I can roll on my back and tummy.

I am looking.

I can see.

You can roll just like me.

Go...Go...Go my mini-me.

Daddy, Daddy, look at me!
I can crawl on my hands and knees.

I am looking.
I can see.
You can crawl just like me.
Go...Go...Go my mini-me.

Daddy, Daddy, look at me!
I can stand on my feet like a tree.

I am looking.

I can see.

You can stand just like me.

Go...Go...Go my mini-me.

Daddy, Daddy, look at me!
I can clap then stomp my feet.

I am looking.

I can see.

You can clap then stomp like me.

Go...Go...Go my mini-me.

Daddy, Daddy, look at me!
I can hug and kiss Mommy.

I am looking.
I can see.
You can hug and kiss like me.
Go...Go...Go my mini-me.

Daddy, Daddy, look at me!
I can wave and say bye-bye.

I am looking.
I can see.
You can do it just like me.
Go...Go...Go my mini-me.

Daddy, Daddy, look at me!
I can brush my two front teeth.

> I am looking.
> I can see.
> You can brush them just like me.
> *Go...Go...Go* my mini-me.

Daddy, Daddy, look at me!
I can use my own potty.

I am looking.

I can see.

You can use it just like me.

Go...Go...Go my mini-me.

Daddy, Daddy, look at me!
I can say my ABC's.

I am looking.
I can see.
You can say them just like me.
Go...Go...Go my mini-me.

Daddy, Daddy, look at me!
I can count up to twenty.

I am looking.

I can see.

You can count them just like me.

Go...Go...Go my mini-me.

Daddy keeps looking as proud as can be.
My Baby will forever look up to me.

My Mini-Me.